LIBRARY SMARTS

STAY SAFE ONLINE

LISA OWINGS

Lerner Publications Company • Minneapolis

Lerner Publications Company
A division of Lerner Publishing Group, Inc.
241 First Avenue North
Minneapolis, MN 55401 U.S.A.

Website address: www.lernerbooks.com

Library of Congress Cataloging-in-Publication Data

Owings, Lisa.
    Stay safe online / by Lisa Owings.
        pages   cm. — (Library smarts)
    Includes index.
    ISBN 978–1–4677–1505–8 (library binding : alkaline paper)
    ISBN 978–1–4677–1754–0 (eBook)
    1. Internet and children—Juvenile literature. 2. Internet—Safety
measures—Juvenile literature. 3. World Wide Web—Safety measures—
Juvenile literature. I. Title.
HQ784.I58O95 2014
004.67'80289—dc23   2013003348

Manufactured in the United States of America
1 – CG – 7/15/13

TABLE OF CONTENTS

The Online World

The online world is fun! You can learn a lot by going online. You can read about all kinds of things. Pictures and videos can help you learn too.

The **Internet** can also be just for fun. You can play games or talk to friends.

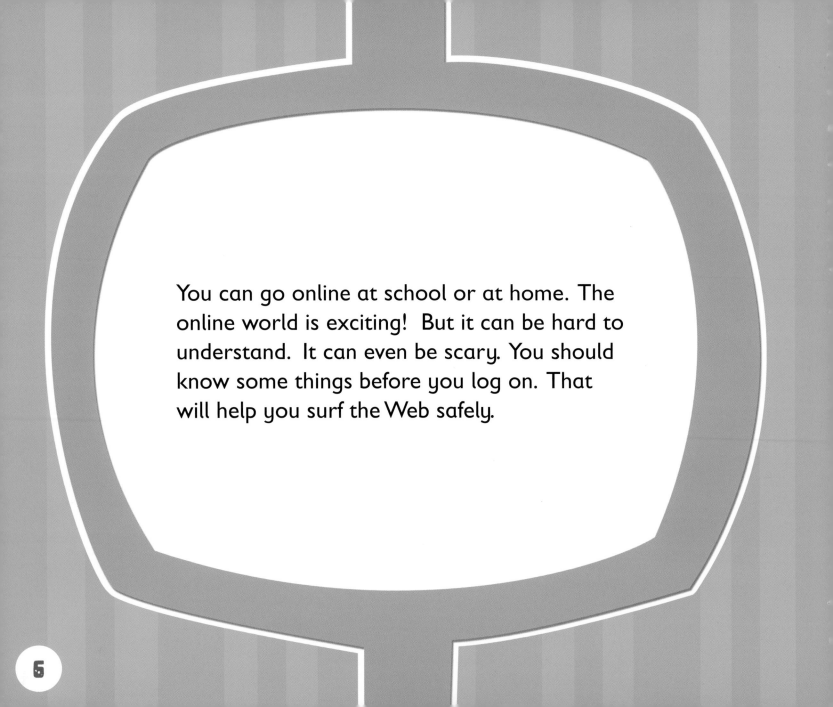

You can go online at school or at home. The online world is exciting! But it can be hard to understand. It can even be scary. You should know some things before you log on. That will help you surf the Web safely.

Smart Web Surfing

Some parts of the Internet are perfect for kids. Others are for adults only. It can be hard to know which parts are which. A parent or a teacher can show you. Stick to the **websites** they say are okay. You'll have more fun that way. *And* you'll stay safe.

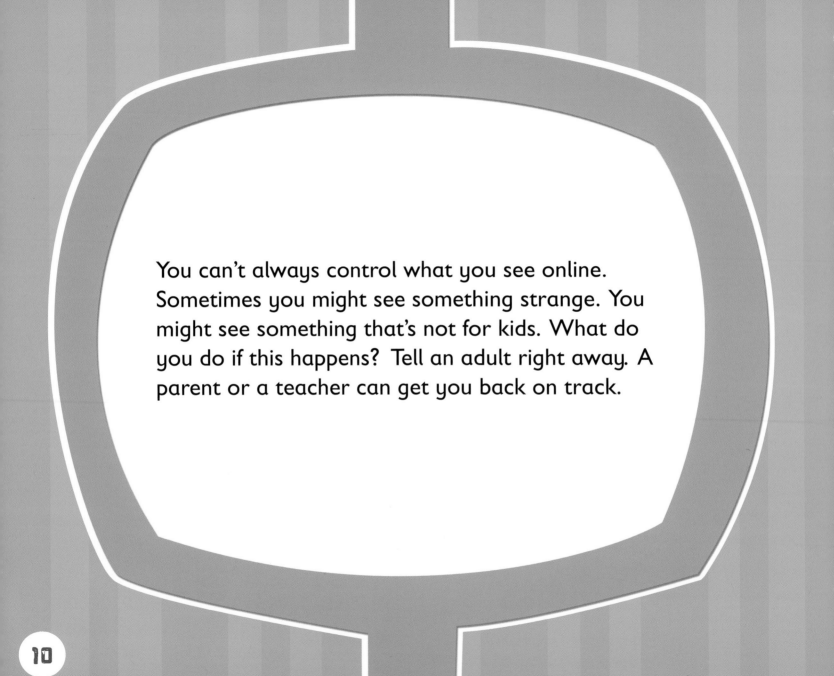

You can't always control what you see online. Sometimes you might see something strange. You might see something that's not for kids. What do you do if this happens? Tell an adult right away. A parent or a teacher can get you back on track.

Guard Your Information

Keep **personal information** secret. Then no one can use it to harm you. Keep your name, address, and birthday to yourself.

Your phone number and your school are personal information too. A site might ask you to share other facts about your life. Always ask an adult first.

A **password** helps keep your secrets safe. It stops others from seeing things meant only for you. You can share passwords with parents or teachers. But never share them with anyone else.

Passwords should be hard to guess. They should have both letters and numbers. They shouldn't have personal information.

Sign in

Username / Email   tjones

Password   ••••••••••••••

SIGN IN

Make Friends Safely

Talking to people online can be fun. Online chatting is great if you're talking to your real-life friends. But what about people you've never met? Those people might not be who they say they are. They might not be your friends at all.

What if a stranger tries to talk to you online? Don't answer. Let a parent or a teacher know.

Don't send pictures to strangers online. And *never* meet a stranger in person.

Sometimes people online do or say mean things. That's called **cyberbullying**. Bullying of any kind is never okay. What if someone online is bullying you? Don't be mean back. Go tell an adult. Say only nice things online. Online remarks can hurt real-life feelings.

The online world is a place to learn. It is a place to have fun. It is also a place to be careful. So remember the rules. Stick to kid-friendly websites. Don't share too much. And don't talk to strangers or bullies. The online world is waiting. Visit it safely!

GLOSSARY

cyberbullying: doing or saying mean things to someone online

Internet: a system of computers that lets people share information

password: a secret code you enter to view certain things on a computer

personal information: facts about who you are and where you live. Personal information can be your name, address, phone number, or other facts.

websites: places on the Internet

INDEX

Photo acknowledgments: The images in this book are used with the permission of: © Hemera/Thinkstock, p. 5; © iStockphoto.com/ Imgorthand, p. 7; © iStockphoto.com/AVAVA, p. 9; © iStockphoto.com/JasonDoiy, p. 11; © iStockphoto.com/Joshua Hodge Photography, pp. 13, 23; © Todd Strand/Independent Picture Service, p. 15; © iStockphoto.com/Margot Petrowski, p. 17; © Larsen & Talbert/Brand X Pictures/Getty Images, p. 19; © Apple Tree House/Riser/Getty Images, p. 21.

Front cover: © Purestock/Thinkstock.

Main body text set in Gill Sans Infant Std Regular 18/22. Typeface provided by Monotype Typography.

24